LEADERSHIP
THAT MAKES AN
IMPACT

BIBLE STUDY GUIDE

A complement to the book

Leadership That Makes an Impact

Carl W. Basden

ISBN 979-8-89112-585-8 (Paperback)
ISBN 979-8-89112-586-5 (Digital)

Copyright © 2024 Carl W. Basden
All rights reserved
First Edition

All rights reserved. No part of this publication may be reproduced, distributed, or transmitted in any form or by any means, including photocopying, recording, or other electronic or mechanical methods without the prior written permission of the publisher. For permission requests, solicit the publisher via the address below.

Covenant Books
11661 Hwy 707
Murrells Inlet, SC 29576
www.covenantbooks.com

INTRODUCTION

Several years ago, I attended an executive education program at Louisiana State University. The instructor in one of the classes asked us to introduce ourselves and, in a word or two, explain our leadership philosophy. I knew integrity was important to me, and that was what I shared. Some of the students had obviously thought this through more than I had, and some even had some acronyms they used to describe their philosophies. I was impressed! I asked myself why I was not able to articulate my thoughts as clearly. I began to work on developing a leadership philosophy, one that I could explain to anyone when called on. I started making a list of the values that were important to me. I wanted it to be practical and easily understood. In addition, I wanted it to be easy to remember.

The book *Leadership That Makes an Impact* shares the outcome of that effort in detail. The book presents a practical leadership model that is easy to understand, remember, and apply. If you have not read the book, I would encourage you to do that before you begin this study. The many stories and points made in that book help establish the importance of the traits in the model. However, this study guide is designed to provide enough context to stand on its own.

The components of the model, forming an acrostic, are as follows:

- **I**ntegrity
- **M**otivation
- **P**erformance
- **A**ttitude
- **C**ommunication
- **T**eamwork

While the model is pretty simple in nature, the consistent application of the values presented can be difficult to perform daily. A natural question is "How can I do these things consistently?"

I'm glad you asked. I can only tell you how it works for me. I am a Christian. The components of the IMPACT model are consistent with Christian principles. If you are a Christian, through this study, I think you will agree the values in the model are supported by Scripture. If you are not a Christian, the model still works. But I invite you to read the chapter titled "How to Become a Christian" in this study guide and consider giving your heart to Jesus. If you approach it with an open mind, these truths can be life-changing. They can make an *everlasting* impact!

You don't have to be a Christian for the model to work. But being a Christian has certainly helped me apply it, and that's because I am not relying on my own power to do it. I am relying on the power of Christ and the inner strength that He gives me.

This model has application for men and women in the workplace. But it will enhance leadership capabilities in any situation. It can be used to strengthen marriage relationships, which are sure to be tested by the challenges of life. Parents can find the model useful as they struggle to find the right approach to leading their children into adulthood.

Many pastors and church administrators are not prepared for the challenges they will face when they assume responsibility for their staff. In addition, they can easily become frustrated with trying to respond to the whims of a demanding congregation and lay leadership. Applying this model will clearly help them navigate some of those rough waters.

A lot of coaches today are thrust into leadership positions because they have excelled at the technicalities of their specific sport. Their win/loss record has made them successful and led to bigger opportunities. Yet they have not had any experience in leading a staff. All of a sudden, they are expected to keep a staff motivated, handle personnel issues, administer discipline in a responsible manner, and still win on the field. Practicing this simple model will help position them to make sound decisions and balance the many expectations.

Does being a Christian automatically make this work? Absolutely not! I could give examples that violate all the values in the model and tell you those violations were performed by leaders who claimed to be Christians. Christians are not perfect! We are just saved sinners! But I can tell you that having the power of Christ in my life makes the practice of this model more achievable.

If you tried, you could find any number of people that could point out my failures, where I did not live up to my own values that I have espoused in the book. I would like to think you could find a few that would indicate that I made a positive impact on their lives and careers, and practicing this model allowed them to see an alignment between my professed Christianity and the way I led the organization.

The purpose of this Bible study guide is to provide a format to discuss the components of the model and examine what the Bible says about those components. The study is designed to promote discussion so that the participants can learn from one another. Practical tips from the examples and illustrations in the book are provided at the conclusion of each lesson. These are intended to serve as simple reminders to help the participant in daily implementation.

I am aware that a lot of the Scripture that is shown in the study guide was written to Christians about how to get along in the church. I am not looking to get into a theological argument or be accused of taking these scriptures out of context. I am simply pointing out that the traits that are discussed in this leadership model are consistent with the qualities that a Christian should display in his/her conduct. And I believe they include how we should act at home and at work. It is especially applicable to how people in leadership positions treat their subordinates.

Actually, there is no better example of what a leader should look like than Jesus Himself. In Mark 10:42–45, Jesus had a discussion with His disciples about leadership.

He explained to them the model they had observed was that a leader was to have power over people and demonstrate dominance. Jesus told them about a different leadership model. The traits of this different type of leader would be a servant and giver, one with humility. He depicted this type leader to be at the bottom of the pyramid, serving others, instead of at the top, lording over them. Servant leadership was a foreign concept to the people in that day when they thought of what a leader should look like. Unfortunately, it is a concept that is still foreign to many leaders today. The servant model that Jesus demonstrated was based on humility and respect for others. People respond positively to that type of leadership! As you participate in this study, I think you will see that the IMPACT model supports those same attributes. Jesus is our example!

If you know Jesus Christ, you are not just in a position to help those who you are responsible for leading, but you are also in a position to impact them for the kingdom of God. That is what God has called us to do!

It is my desire that you find this study guide and this leadership model to be blessings to you! My prayer is that they will be used to strengthen your leadership capabilities as you develop in your role. Whether your leadership role is in your career, your church, or your family, displaying the qualities described herein can improve your effectiveness. Be thankful for the position in which God has entrusted you!

Now let us go make an impact!

INTEGRITY

What are some words that you think about to describe integrity?

____

____

____

____

What does the Bible say about integrity?

- Integrity in our daily lives
    - *Daniel 1:7–9*
    - How did Daniel show integrity?
    - He would not _______________ himself by sinning against his God.
    - He purposed in his heart. He made up his mind.
    - It is wise to decide in advance that we will not _______________ our integrity.
    - *Proverbs 10:9*
- Integrity in our home lives
    - *Genesis 39:10–12*
    - How did Joseph show integrity?
    - He fled. He _______________ himself from the situation.

- ○ He did not resist because Potiphar might find out.
  - ○ He _________________ because he could not have _________________ with himself.
  - ○ *Proverbs 20:7*
- Integrity in our work/leadership roles
  - ○ *1 Samuel 12:1–5*
  - ○ How did Samuel show integrity?
  - ○ He had not _________________ them.
  - ○ He had not taken _________________.
  - ○ He had not _________________ them.
  - ○ *Proverbs 22:1*

Discussion Questions

How do you feel when you hear people say one thing and do another?

____

____

Has there been a situation where your integrity was questioned?

____

____

Has there been a time where you were faced with an ethical dilemma?

____

____

What do you do when you need to admit your mistakes?

____

____

Practical Tips

- Tell the truth.
- Avoid compromising your values.
- Follow through on promises you make.
- Practice ethical conduct.
- Ensure consistency in your talk and your walk.
- Make up your mind in advance not to violate what you know to be right.
- Refrain from sharing confidential information with others.
- Remain honest with your partner.
- Avoid gossiping about other people.
- Admit when you are wrong.

MOTIVATION

What characteristic of a leader has inspired you in the workplace?

____

____

____

____

What does the Bible say about motivation?

- We first must examine ourselves.
  - *Psalm 40:8*—David was motivated by his _______________ desire. Our first priority should be to do the will of the Father. We should want our work to honor Him.
  - *John 4:34*—Jesus set the _______________ for us. He had a hunger to do the will of the Father.
  - *Philippians 1:21*—Paul demonstrated how to remain motivated in difficult times. How a leader responds personally to challenges greatly affects how the team will be motivated to work through those challenges. The leader sets the _______________.

- We can then focus on how to best motivate others.
    - *1 Thessalonians 5:11*—Our goal should be to _____________ one another, to build one another up. To do that, we must care for others.
    - If we genuinely care about people, treating them right will come naturally, and they will much more likely be motivated.
    - *2 Timothy 4:2*—Paul instructed these Christians how to treat one another. He told them to be urgent in exhorting and coaching but to do it with _____________. People normally respond positively to someone who is willing to _____________ in them.

Discussion Questions

How do you motivate yourself to fulfill your responsibilities?

____
____

What factors tend to keep you from being personally motivated?

____
____

What is the best way to motivate someone else? What has worked for you?

____

____

How do you ensure that everyone understands the direction you are leading them to go?

____

____

How do you demonstrate to people that you genuinely care about them?

____

____

Practical Tips

- Embrace opportunity.
- Provide focus and direction.
- Lead with empathy.
- Have fun.
- Genuinely care. *It's about people!*
- Value and respect every team member.
- Utilize two powerful words: *thank you*!

PERFORMANCE

How much value is placed on performance evaluations where you work?

____

____

____

____

What does the Bible say about performance?

- Work hard and cheerfully.
  - *Colossians 3:23*—We must respect those who have been put in authority over us. Our _________________ respect should be to God, and we should resolve to honor Him in our approach to work. We should be a _________________ for our coworkers. They should be able to see that a Christian gives his/her best effort because of his/her desire to honor God. After all, He gave us His best.
- Work for God's glory.
  - *1 Corinthians 10:31*—Paul was teaching the Corinthian Christians about the freedom they enjoyed in Christ. He wanted their

___________________, whatever they did, to be for the glory of God. That should be our goal as Christians—to glorify God in all we do. It should include our approach to work. People are watching us, and they are quick to see if there is _______________ in our claim as Christians and our conduct.

- Follow through on commitments.
  - *Proverbs 14:23*—Talk is cheap. In many instances, there is too much talk and not enough _______________. J. Vernon McGee says that people can be classified as "talking" people or "doing" people. Following through on commitments is essential. That is especially true for Christians because we are _______________ the Lord.

Discussion Questions

How do you instill within an organization the desire to win?

____

____

How do you lead a team to improve their performance?

____

____

What is the key to ensuring your organization achieves the desired results?

____

____

Can a total focus on performance cause us to treat people wrongly? Can it cause us to compromise our integrity—for example, cheat?

____

____

How can we expect improved performance and treat others right at the same time?

____

____

Practical Tips

- Commit to win!
- Drive for results; be determined to reach goals.
- Set expectations and hold people accountable.
- Display a sense of urgency.
- Utilize humor effectively.
- Expect operational excellence.
- Follow through on commitments.
- Pay attention to detail.
- Prioritize appropriately.

ATTITUDE

How would you describe the perfect work environment?

____

____

____

____

What does the Bible say about attitude?

- Attitude of Christlikeness
  - *Philippians 2:5–7*—Jesus was a _______. Jesus was fully God, but He "emptied" Himself so that He could carry out the will of God. He was the Son of God, clearly having ________________, but He humbled Himself and served others. What an example for us! Some leaders are consumed with power and do not get the need to humble themselves.
- Attitude of joy
  - *Philippians 4:4*—Regardless of the situation, Paul said the Christian has reason to express joy. Paul actually issued it as a ________________. It is a fruit of the Spirit, so we are empowered to do it.

- Attitude of perseverance
  - *Galatians 6:9*—When the difficult times come, we can be ________________ to give up. Paul said, "Don't give up." He used the illustration of a farmer and declared that we will reap what we sow. He challenged us to keep sowing goodness.
- Attitude of humility
  - *1 Peter 5:5*—We have already looked at how Jesus demonstrated humility. Peter underscored the importance of humility. We have all seen leaders who were consumed with their own ________________. God resists the proud and gives grace to the humble. Clothe yourself in humility and receive God's grace.

Discussion Questions

What part does attitude play in a leader's success?

____

____

Have you ever had a time where you wanted to give up but chose not to?

____

____

How do you respond when you are around negative conversations?

____

____

How do you handle it when you feel overwhelmed?

____

____

How do you handle it when changes come your way?

____

____

Practical Tips

- Be responsible for your own attitude; don't allow someone else to control it.
- Be positive.
- Expect a "can do" attitude.
- Practice humility.
- Be willing to laugh at yourself.
- Get personally involved.
- Embrace change.

COMMUNICATION

How would you describe good, effective communication?

____

____

____

____

What does the Bible say about communication?

- Communicate in a way that builds up.
  - *Ephesians 4:29*—Paul was challenging the Christians at Ephesus to make sure their _______________ was healthy for growing in unity. These instructions are also very practical for us in the workplace. When the stress level is high at work, it is easy to forget who we belong to and fly off the handle or say things we will later regret. The workplace also tempts Christians to fall into filthy conversation. _______________ matter! We need to be cognizant of our witness and make sure we are building it up and not tearing it down.

- Communication includes listening.
  - ○ *James 1:19–20*—We have all heard it said that God gave us two ears and one mouth for a reason. James was encouraging his readers to hear the Word of God. We should too and allow it to teach us. The principle also applies to how we _________________ with others. People want to be heard, and we should take time to _________________.
- Communicate in a manner that pleases God.
  - ○ *Psalm 19:14*—This is such a practical prayer by the psalmist David. If we incorporate this prayer into our daily lives, it can have a profound effect on how we communicate with others.

Discussion Questions

How do you ensure that people understand what has been communicated?

____

____

What communication techniques have proved to be effective for you?

____

____

If someone can talk a lot, does that make them a good communicator?

____

____

What are the greatest challenges to effective communication?

____

____

How has the development of Internet and social media changed the way we communicate?

____

____

Practical Tips

- Leaders must be able to communicate.
- Communicate clearly. Remember, it is easy to be misunderstood.
- Don't assume they know.
- Build one another up.
- Communicate truthfully.
- Remember to listen.
- Close the feedback loop.

TEAMWORK

What is the greatest example of teamwork you have observed?

____

____

____

____

What does the Bible say about teamwork?

- We need a helper.
  - *Genesis 2:18*—Many people think they are invincible and can accomplish everything on their own. J. Vernon McGee said that there is a reason that God placed Adam in the garden _________________ for a period of time. It was to show him that he had a need. He needed someone to be with him. Nowhere is the need for teamwork more evident than in the _________________ relationship. We need each other! We work better together! Marriage teaches us to carry our part of the load and share the responsibility.

- Teamwork makes us better.
  - *Proverbs 27:17*—It is so good to have a team-mate with whom to brainstorm ideas. We need ________________. We gain strength from one another. We need to depend on one another. It is true in our marriages, it is true in our spiritual growth journeys, and it is true in relationships at work. We make one another better! ________________ support one another, care for one another, and may be forced to defend one another.
- Teamwork allows us to accomplish more.
  - *Ecclesiastes 4:9–10*—Solomon discovered that there was benefit in teaming up to ________________ a task. There was more to be gained when they worked together. It is good to have someone who can pick you up when you fall. We learn from one another! Teamwork ________________success!

Discussion Questions

How do you make sure that everyone is pulling in the same direction?

____

____

What things can you do to ensure that every team member knows they are important?

____

____

How do you deal with a team member who does not practice teamwork?

____

____

What do you expect of existing team members when new members join?

____

____

How do you motivate team members who are disengaged?

____

____

Practical Tips

- Teamwork drives success!
- Value every team member.
- We learn from one another.
- Take the initiative to help your teammates.

HOW TO BECOME
A CHRISTIAN

I grew up in a small rural community in North Mississippi. I went to church with my parents from the time that I was born. When I was fifteen years old, I confessed my sins and invited Jesus Christ into my heart. While I was not a bad person, I recognized that I was a sinner and in need of a Savior. I am so appreciative of God's grace and His wonderful love for me. He loved me so much that He gave His only Son to die in my place. Trusting Christ to save me was the best decision that I have ever made. Since that time, I have tried to walk with Him and live a life that would honor Him. He has blessed me immensely. The Holy Spirit lives inside me! If I rely on Him and not on myself, He guides me in the practice of the values in the model and helps me make a positive impact on the people I have the privilege of leading. Jesus provides purpose and meaning to my life! And He can to your life, too!

If you have never placed your trust in Christ, I encourage you to do that today. The Bible makes it very clear that man is a sinner (Romans 3:23). The price for sin is death (Romans 6:23). God loved us so much that He gave His only Son to pay the price for our sin (John 3:16). He sent

Jesus to die on the cross in our place (Romans 5:8). The Bible says that if you confess that you are a sinner and you believe that Jesus died for you and rose again, you can ask Him to save you, and He will do it (Romans 10:9–10).

Making this decision can dramatically change your life and your perspective in dealing with people. People need leaders who are willing to respect and invest in them. If you have made the decision to follow Jesus, you are now the complete person that God designed you to be. You are now in the best position to make a positive impact on others for the glory of God!

⸎

ANSWER KEY TO STATEMENTS LISTED IN EACH TOPIC

Integrity

What does the Bible say about integrity?

- Integrity in our daily lives
  - *Daniel 1:7–9*
  - How did Daniel show integrity?
  - He would not *defile* himself by sinning against his God.
  - He purposed in his heart. He made up his mind.
  - It is wise to decide in advance that we will not *compromise* our integrity.
  - *Proverbs 10:9*
- Integrity in our home lives
  - *Genesis 39:10–12*
  - How did Joseph show integrity?
  - He fled. He *removed* himself from the situation.
  - He did not resist because Potiphar might find out.

- ○ He *resisted* because he could not have *lived* with himself.
  - ○ *Proverbs 20:7*
- Integrity in our work/leadership roles
  - ○ *1 Samuel 12:1–5*
  - ○ How did Samuel show integrity?
  - ○ He had not *wronged* them.
  - ○ He had not taken *bribes.*
  - ○ He had not *oppressed* them.
  - ○ *Proverbs 22:1*

Motivation

What does the Bible say about motivation?

- We first must examine ourselves.
  - ○ *Psalm 40:8*—David was motivated by his *heart's* desire. Our first priority should be to do the will of the Father. We should want our work to honor Him.
  - ○ *John 4:34.* Jesus set the *example* for us. He had a hunger to do the will of the Father.
  - ○ *Philippians 1:21*—Paul demonstrated how to remain motivated in difficult times. How a leader responds personally to challenges greatly affects how the team will be motivated to work through those challenges. The leader sets the *tone.*

- We can then focus on how to best motivate others.
  - *1 Thessalonians 5:11*—Our goal should be to *encourage* one another, to build one another up. To do that, we must care for others.
  - If we genuinely care about people, treating them right will come naturally, and they will much more likely be motivated.
  - *2 Timothy 4:2*—Paul instructed these Christians how to treat one another. He told them to be urgent in exhorting and coaching but to do it with *patience*. People normally respond positively to someone who is willing to *invest* in them.

Performance

What does the Bible say about performance?

- Work hard and cheerfully.
  - *Colossians 3:23*—We must respect those who have been put in authority over us. Our *utmost* respect should be to God, and we should resolve to honor Him in our approach to work. We should be a *model* for our coworkers. They should be able to see that a Christian gives his/her best effort because of his/her desire to honor God. After all, He gave us His best.
- Work for God's glory.
  - *1 Corinthians 10:31*—Paul was teaching the Corinthian Christians about the freedom they

enjoyed in Christ. He wanted their *conduct*, whatever they did, to be for the glory of God. That should be our goal as Christians—to glorify God in all we do. It should include our approach to work. People are watching us, and they are quick to see if there is *consistency* in our claim as Christians and our conduct.

- Follow through on commitments.
  - *Proverbs 14:23*—Talk is cheap. In many instances, there is too much talk and not enough *execution*. J. Vernon McGee says that people can be classified as "talking" people or "doing" people. Following through on commitments is essential. That is especially true for Christians because we are *representing* the Lord.

Attitude

What does the Bible say about attitude?

- Attitude of Christlikeness
  - *Philippians 2:5–7*—Jesus was a *servant*. Jesus was fully God, but He "emptied" Himself so that He could carry out the will of God. He was the Son of God, clearly having *power*, but He humbled Himself and served others. What an example for us! Some leaders are consumed with power and do not get the need to humble themselves.

- Attitude of joy
  - *Philippians 4:4*—Regardless of the situation, Paul said the Christian has reason to express joy. Paul actually issued it as a *command*. It is a fruit of the Spirit, so we are empowered to do it.
- Attitude of perseverance
  - *Galatians 6:9*—When the difficult times come, we can be *tempted* to give up. Paul said, "Don't give up." He used the illustration of a farmer and declares we will reap what we sow. He challenged us to keep sowing goodness.
- Attitude of humility
  - *1 Peter 5:5*—We have already looked at how Jesus demonstrated humility. Peter underscored the importance of humility. We have all seen leaders who were consumed with their own *importance*. God resists the proud and gives grace to the humble. Clothe yourself in humility and receive God's grace.

Communication

What does the Bible say about communication?

- Communicate in a way that builds up.
  - *Ephesians 4:29*—Paul was challenging the Christians at Ephesus to make sure their *conversation* was healthy for growing in unity. The instructions are also very practical for us in

the workplace. When the stress level is high at work, it is easy to forget who we belong to and fly off the handle or say things we will later regret. The workplace also tempts Christians to fall into filthy conversation. *Words* matter! We need to be cognizant of our witness and make sure we are building it up and not tearing it down.

- Communication includes listening.
  - *James 1:19–20*—We have all heard it said that God gave us two ears and one mouth for a reason. James was encouraging his readers to hear the Word of God. We should too and allow it to teach us. The principle also applies to how we *communicate* with others. People want to be heard, and we should take time to *listen.*
- Communicate in a manner that pleases God.
  - *Psalm 19:14*—This is such a practical prayer by the psalmist David. If we incorporate this prayer into our daily lives, it can have a profound effect on how we communicate with others.

Teamwork

What does the Bible say about teamwork?

- We need a helper.
  - *Genesis 2:18*—Many people think they are invincible and can accomplish everything on

their own. J. Vernon McGee said that there is a reason that God placed Adam in the garden *alone* for a period of time. It was to show him that he had a need. He needed someone to be with him. Nowhere is the need for teamwork more evident than in the *marriage* relationship. We need each other! We work better together! Marriage teaches us to carry our part of the load and share the responsibility.

- Teamwork makes us better.
  - *Proverbs 27:17*—It is so good to have a teammate with whom to brainstorm ideas. We need *accountability*. We gain strength from one another. We need to depend on one another. It is true in our marriages, it is true in our spiritual growth journeys, and it is true in relationships at work. We make one another better! *Teammates* support one another, care for one another, and may be forced to defend one another.
- Teamwork allows us to accomplish more.
  - *Ecclesiastes 4:9–10*—Solomon discovered that there was benefit in teaming up to *accomplish* a task. There was more to be gained when they worked together. It is good to have someone who can pick you up when you fall. We learn from one another! Teamwork *drives* success!

ABOUT THE AUTHOR

**Carl Basden spent** his career in telecommunications with South Central Bell, BellSouth, and AT&T. As an assistant vice president, he led large organizations with responsibilities in engineering, construction, installation, and maintenance. After retiring from AT&T, he worked for four years as a division vice president with MasTec Inc.

Carl is a native of Mississippi. He holds a bachelor's degree in civil engineering from Mississippi State University and an MBA from Mississippi College. After living and working in a number of places throughout the South, Carl and his wife, Sharia, currently reside in Starkville, Mississippi. They have three children and a growing number of grandchildren.

Serving the Lord and being involved in the local church have always been priorities for Carl and Sharia. He has taught Bible study groups for most of his adult life, and he has served in various leadership capacities. He has served as board chairman for the Mississippi State University chapter of the Fellowship of Christian Athletes. Sharia has worked with children's choirs in the many churches of which they have been members.

www.ingramcontent.com/pod-product-compliance
Lightning Source LLC
Chambersburg PA
CBHW031006180726
47993CB00018B/1584